SUPERSTARS

of

PRO FOOTBALL

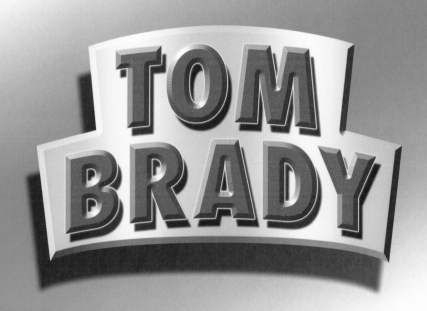

TOM BRADY

Calvin Craig Miller

Mason Crest Publishers

Produced by OTTN Publishing in association with
21st Century Publishing and Communications, Inc.

MASON CREST PUBLISHERS INC.
370 Reed Road
Broomall, Pennsylvania 19008
(866) MCP-BOOK (toll free)
www.masoncrest.com

Printed in the United States of America.

First Printing

9 8 7 6 5 4 3 2 1

Library of Congress Cataloging-in-Publication Data

Miller, Calvin Craig, 1954–
    Tom Brady / Calvin Craig Miller.
        p. cm. — (Superstars of pro football)
ISBN 978-1-4222-0539-6 (hardcover) — ISBN 978-1-4222-0820-5 (pbk.)
    1. Brady, Tom, 1977–   —Juvenile literature. 2. Football players—United
States—Biography—Juvenile literature. I. Title.
GV939.B685M55 2008
796.332092—dc22
[B]   2008025392

Publisher's note:
All quotations in this book come from original sources, and contain the spelling
and grammatical inconsistencies of the original text.

◀◀ CROSS-CURRENTS ▶▶

In the ebb and flow of the currents of life we are each influenced
by many people, places, and events that we directly experience or
have learned about. Throughout the chapters of this book you will
come across **CROSS-CURRENTS** reference bubbles. These bubbles
direct you to a **CROSS-CURRENTS** section in the back of the
book that contains fascinating and informative sidebars
and related pictures. Go on. ▶▶

◄◄CONTENTS►►

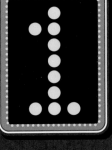

GREATEST IN THE GAME

When Tom Brady won the National Football League's 2007 Most Valuable Player (MVP) Award, he did not have much competition. Out of 50 media judges, only one did not vote for Tom. Few who had seen the New England Patriots quarterback on field could doubt that he was a once-in-a-lifetime player who had helped lift his team to greatness.

Patriots team owner Robert Kraft had seen firsthand the difference Tom made in New England. He told an Associated Press reporter,

❝To be honest, I'm surprised it took so long for him to get this recognition because he's sort of been our

During the 2007 season, Tom Brady had one of the best seasons by a quarterback in NFL history. As a result, the New England Patriots superstar was named the league's Most Valuable Player.

MVP since he stepped on the field in '01. . . . And the thing that I've found most interesting is if you talk to role players or backups how he talks to them and motivates them. He treats them like they're going to the Pro Bowl, with that kind of respect. **99**

Leader of the Powerful Patriots

Tom was a spectacular quarterback in 2007, leading one of the greatest teams in the history of the National Football League. At the time of the MVP vote, the Patriots had just finished an unbeaten regular season, rolling over all 16 of their opponents.

By doing this, the Patriots had broken an **NFL** record that had stood for 35 years. The last team to go unbeaten through their regular season had been the 1972 Miami Dolphins, who won all 14 of their regular-season games on the way to a victory in Super Bowl VII.

Tom had helped New England put 589 points on the scoreboard, an NFL record. The team scored a record 75 **touchdowns**. On the strength of his passing arm, he had churned out 4,806 yards and an amazing 50 touchdown passes. This set another new NFL record. Tom's passing accuracy helped his teammate Randy Moss set his own NFL record, with 23 touchdown catches.

CROSS-CURRENTS

Read "Undefeated Dolphins" to learn about the only team in history to complete an undefeated season with a Super Bowl win. Go to page 48. ▶▶

An Outstanding Career

Few football fans were surprised that the Patriots were a dominant team in 2007. During Tom's eight-year professional career, New England had always been one of the National Football League's best teams. Tom had led the Patriots to three Super Bowl victories. He had twice been named Most Valuable Player for the Super Bowl.

For years Tom had been considered one of the NFL's best quarterbacks. By the end of the 2007 season, many people were saying that he was one of the best quarterbacks ever to play the game. He was compared to other former league MVPs who were now in pro football's Hall of Fame, such as Johnny Unitas, Bart Starr, John Elway, and Tom's own childhood hero, Joe Montana.

Tom fires a pass downfield during a 2007 game against the Dallas Cowboys. During the 2007 season, Tom threw for over 4,800 yards and set a league record with 50 touchdown passes.

Tom modestly downplayed such comparisons. He told reporters that he was proud to be named the MVP. He said that people should wait until his career ended before comparing him to the all-time greats. Tom told the Associated Press,

> **"I have always been a huge football fan and will always have great respect for the history of this game. I am flattered to join such an esteemed list of players, many of whom I consider the greatest of all time. I hope that I can set as great of an example for kids around the world as the previous MVPs did for me."**

Respected by His Teammates

Tom's job is to lead the Patriots' **offense**, the unit of the team that attempts to score, either with touchdowns or **field goals**. The

As the leader of New England's offense, Tom (number 12) helped the Patriots break the NFL record for most points scored in the regular season. The team scored 589 points in 2007—an average of nearly 37 points per game.

defense has to keep the offense of the other team from scoring. The units are not on the field at the same time. Yet even defensive players among the Patriots gave Tom some credit for their success, because they played against him in practice. Linebacker Mike Vrabel said,

> **He's our MVP. I think we've known that for quite some time. I think his work ethic day in and day out [is most impressive]. We get to practice against him, so I think that makes us better. I think it makes us a better defense. He puts a lot of time into it. It's important to him. Going out there every week and then trying to play his absolute best is a priority for him.**

Patriots coach Bill Belichick is not one who easily or often hands out praise. He can be hard on his players, and is often more prone to finding weak points in a victory than celebrating it. Yet he knew well how Tom had helped lift New England from being a middle-of-the-pack squad to being the NFL's most dominant team. When he heard that Tom had been chosen the NFL's Most Valuable Player in 2007, Belichick said:

> **He deserves it. I have thought for a long time that there is no past or present quarterback I'd rather coach than Tom Brady, and I am more certain of that every year he plays.**

A Hard Worker

Tom Brady has not always been a great athlete, but he has always been a competitor. He has had to struggle for a place on every football team since his high-school years. Often in his career, people thought he was too frail to handle football's brutal hits and hard tackles. He has had to prove his doubters wrong, ever since he was just a little kid watching in fascination as men hurled a football down a hundred-yard field in a championship game.

QUARTERBACK DREAMS

Misery is one thing Tom Brady recalls about the first pro football game he remembers attending. He started crying when his parents refused to buy him one of the big foam "Number 1" fingers that fans waved at San Francisco 49ers home games. He was only four, and tantrums are not unusual for a toddler.

The thing Tom says he remembers most clearly, though, was the spectacular play of the 49ers—especially their quarterback, Joe Montana. After bawling for almost the entire first half, Tom began to pay attention to what was happening on the field. It was a playoff game in January 1982, and the winner would play in Super Bowl XVI. With the Dallas Cowboys leading, everyone in the stadium wondered if Montana could stage a last-minute comeback. The 49ers star came through in the clutch. With Cowboy defenders chasing him, he floated a touchdown pass into the arms of 49ers receiver Dwight Clark.

Tom did not understand all of the action on the field, but he heard the way the crowd cheered the players. He later said this was the first time he thought about playing professional football.

CROSS-CURRENTS

To learn more about the San Francisco 49ers quarterback that Tom Brady idolized growing up, read "Joe Montana." Go to page 48. ▶▶

Tom Brady grew up in a large, close-knit family. When he was growing up, family activities were common. "I have a special relationship with my parents and sisters because of all that time we spent together," Tom said in 2002.

Sports Family

Tom came from the right family for such dreams. His father, Tom Brady Sr., and his mother, Galynn, both loved sports. Tom was born on August 3, 1977, in San Mateo, a small city just south of San Francisco. The Bradys were devout Catholics who faithfully attended Sunday Mass.

Tom and Galynn Brady encouraged all their children to play sports. Tom's sisters Maureen, Julie, and Nancy played softball and soccer. In fact, the girls helped Tom develop as an athlete, allowing him to play with older kids in their neighborhood. Nancy later told writer Charles P. Pierce:

> **"I don't think we were typical girls. I think we all liked to play everything the boys did, and there were about eighty or ninety kids in the neighborhood, so there was always something going on. And it was always the three Brady girls and Tommy."**

Tom liked all sports, but he did not seem like a natural football player. He played in neighborhood pickup games, but he was always a skinny kid. If his friends had been playing tackle football instead of touch football, Tom would have gotten clobbered.

When he attended St. Gregory's, a Catholic elementary school, he played basketball and baseball. St. Gregory's did not have a football team. He had to put his quarterback ambitions on hold until he enrolled in Junípero Serra High School.

High School Sports Star

Tom played baseball and football at Junípero Serra. In his junior year, 1993–94, Tom became the starting quarterback for the Padres. Over the next two seasons he earned national attention, throwing for more than 3,500 yards and 33 touchdowns. He was chosen for the All-State Team, and named an All-American player by magazines like *Blue Chip Illustrated* and *Prep Football Report*.

Tom was also a very good baseball player. He played catcher, and was so good that some Major League Baseball teams became interested in him. The Montreal Expos even chose Tom in the 18th round of the 1995 draft.

Tom considered the offer, but decided that he wanted to go to college and play football. He and his parents sent tapes of his high school games to the coaches at Division I schools. Almost all of them showed interest. This meant Tom could choose from some of the best college football programs in the country.

Tom decided to attend the University of Michigan, a school with a long tradition of great football teams. Every year Michigan attracted some of the best football players in the country. Some of them were quarterbacks, so Tom would have to work hard to earn a starting spot on the team. However, Tom understood that if he wanted to be a great quarterback, he would have to test himself against other great players.

Fighting for a Chance to Play

When Tom started school at Michigan in the fall of 1995, there were six other quarterbacks on the team. In his freshman year, Coach Lloyd Carr **redshirted** Tom. This meant he was allowed to practice with the team, but could not play in games. Tom had to watch from the sidelines as another freshman, Scott Dreisbach, battled with sophomore Brian Griese for the starting quarter-back's job. He began to wonder if he had made the right decision in choosing a school where he might see so little playing time.

In Tom's sophomore year, 1996, he thought he had played well enough in training camp to win the starting job. He was again disappointed when Coach Carr named Griese the starter. Tom had always been a team player, but he was frustrated. He told the coach that he was thinking of transferring to another university. Coach Carr urged him to be patient.

CROSS-CURRENTS

Michigan has one of the most famous programs in Division I college football. To learn more, read "Wolverines Football." Go to page 50. ▶▶

Tom earned a little more playing time in his junior year. In four games, he completed 12 of 15 passes for 103 yards. Then he suffered another setback, when he had to be hospitalized for a severe case of appendicitis. He went back to the sidelines.

Although Tom was not having much fun, the Wolverines were playing great football in 1997. Behind Griese, who was now a senior, Michigan went unbeaten during the regular season, then beat Washington State in the Rose Bowl. That gave Michigan a share of the national championship.

Tom Brady (number 10) runs for a first down at the Citrus Bowl, January 1999. In Tom's two seasons at Michigan, the Wolverines were ranked among the nation's top football teams. They finished 10-3 in 1998 and 10-2 in 1999.

Becoming the Starter

Griese's graduation finally gave Tom the opportunity he had been waiting for. He turned in a stellar performance in training. Carr announced that Tom would be the starter.

The 1998 season did not begin well. The Wolverines lost their first game to Notre Dame. When they stumbled to a second defeat against Syracuse, Tom sensed his career might be in trouble. But showing his leadership ability, he encouraged his teammates to turn things around. After that early season crisis, the Wolverines rolled through opponents. Michigan won all but one of its remaining games, and tied for the Big Ten championship. In their Citrus Bowl matchup against Arkansas, Tom pulled the offense together for a come-from-behind victory.

In 1999, his last year at Michigan, Tom faced yet another competition for the starting job. This time, his rival was Drew Henson, a talented all-around athlete who had turned down a chance to play baseball for the New York Yankees in order to play for the Wolverines. Henson had grown up near Ann Arbor, where the University of Michigan was located, so he was a local hero. Many fans badly wanted to see him play for the team.

Coach Carr decided to rotate quarterbacks, starting Brady in the first quarter and Henson in the second. At halftime, whichever player had performed the best would get to finish the game. At first, the Wolverines won games. But then Henson made some mistakes that contributed to two straight losses. Coach Carr announced that Brady would be the full-time starter again.

With the final quarterback dilemma of his college career behind him, Brady confidently took control of the Wolverines. He led the team to a string of victories that resulted in an invitation to the Orange Bowl. Michigan won the game thanks to a record-breaking performance by Tom. His 46 passing **attempts**, 31 **completions**, 369 passing yards, and four touchdowns all set new marks.

The Orange Bowl victory was a brilliant end to Tom's college career. Michigan had won 20 of 25 games that Tom had started. He had shown that he could keep his cool even when his team was losing, and had often led the Wolverines to comeback wins. He had proven that he was one of the best college quarterbacks. But now Tom would face another obstacle. He would learn how difficult it can be for even the best college players to break into the National Football League.

UNDERDOG CHAMPIONS

On April 20, 2000, the Brady family gathered around the television set to watch a broadcast of the annual NFL **draft**. At the draft, pro football teams take turns choosing the country's best young players. Tom's family was sure he would be picked in the early rounds of the draft. He had shown that he was a winner.

However, the early rounds came and went without Tom's name being called. Frustrated, he finally decided that he could not endure watching any longer. He left the house and went to see a San Francisco Giants baseball game.

When Tom returned, his name still had not been called. His sister Nancy later told an interviewer,

The newest member of the New England Patriots jogs during a team practice, 2000. Tom was disappointed not to be chosen in the early rounds of the 2000 NFL draft. However, he was happy to be picked by the Patriots.

"He was really disappointed. By then, my sisters and I were just watching the names on the ticker and saying 'Okay, so who's he?'"

The draft spilled into a second day, and hours went by as lesser players—as least as the Brady family saw it—were drafted into the professional ranks. Tom went out for an angry walk. While he was gone, the phone rang. It was Bill Belichick, the coach of the New England Patriots.

Tom's father took the call. He did not want to tell an interested NFL coach that his son had left the house during the draft, so he said that Tom was in the shower. His family quickly got Tom back to the house so that he could talk to Belichick. Before the day ended, the Patriots had drafted Tom. Tom had wanted to be selected earlier—he was the 199th player chosen—but at least he had made the cut.

CROSS-CURRENTS

Today, Bill Belichick is one of the NFL's most respected coaches. To read more about him, see "Coach Belichick." Go to page 50. ▶▶

Back on the Bench

No sooner had he signed a contract with New England than he found himself waging yet another battle for playing time. He arrived at the team's home at Foxboro, Massachusetts, as the fourth quarterback. The starter was Drew Bledsoe, who had led the Patriots to the 1997 Super Bowl. For the time being, Tom was content to take the backup role. He set his sights on what he considered an achievable goal—becoming the first backup to Bledsoe.

He studied hard, with his usual attention to detail. Before he even got to Foxboro, he had memorized the team's playbook. And Tom was so confident, he even dared to tell team owner Robert Kraft that the team had been wise to draft him. One day, as he was leaving practice with a pizza under his arm, Tom saw Kraft leaving his office. Kraft recalled:

CROSS-CURRENTS

To learn more about the history of the team that drafted Tom, read "The New England Patriots." Go to page 52. ▶▶

"So this skinny beanpole guy walks out, and he comes up to me, and he says, 'Mr. Kraft? I'm Tom Brady.

Tom (right) practices with a teammate during the Patriots' 2000 training camp. When Tom joined the team, New England already had three other quarterbacks. Tom worked hard so he would be ready when he got a chance to play.

Injured New England quarterback Drew Bledsoe (wearing headset) meets Tom on the sidelines after an offensive series, 2001. Tom was thrust into the starting role when Bledsoe went down during the second game of the 2001 season.

We haven't met yet, but I'm the best decision this **franchise** has ever made.' And it was weird the way he said it, you know? It wasn't like he was arrogant, but it was more like he was very confident."

At first, his teammates were not impressed with this late-round pick for a crowded contest at quarterback. When Tom took off his shirt, they thought he was the scrawniest pro football player they had ever seen. They even teased Tom about his skinny appearance. Tom took the ribbing in stride.

Moving up on the Depth Chart

The Patriots won only five games during Tom's rookie year. Tom practiced harder than ever during the off-season. He lifted weights to add to his strength and did practice drills to improve his arm. He added fifteen pounds to his frame and began throwing the ball farther in practice.

In turn, the competition dwindled at the quarterback position. One player left the team, leaving Tom, Michael Bishop, and Damon Huard fighting it out for the number-two spot. The Patriots dropped Bishop, kept Huard at number three, and announced that Tom would be the backup. Tom thought the patience he had learned playing backup at Michigan had paid off. He later talked about the importance of always being prepared, so that he could make the most of any chances he got:

"You go through times in college, even those first three years [at Michigan] that I wasn't playing, hey, I was ready to play even if the coach didn't put me in—so when he put me in my fourth year, I was ready to go. The same thing happened here."

Tom may have been optimistic, but the New England sports writers weren't. They had predicted that the Patriots would not be good in 2001. At first, it seemed they were right. New England lost its first two games. In the second, a home matchup against the New York Jets, Drew Bledsoe suffered the kind of dreadful injury that can have a whole stadium crowd holding its breath. In the fourth quarter, Jets

Tom scrambles while looking downfield for a receiver during an October 2001 game against the San Diego Chargers. Tom learned and improved each week that he played. He helped New England earn a playoff spot that season.

linebacker Mo Lewis dropped a punishing hit on Bledsoe, and he went to the ground. The hit from Lewis sheared a blood vessel in Bledsoe's chest. The quarterback had to be helped off the field.

Tom Brady was put into the game. Although he did OK, he was not able to establish much of a rhythm against the Jets, who won the game. But in the team's next game, against the Indianapolis Colts, Tom coolly took over. He led the Patriots to their best showing in the early season, a 44-13 blowout.

Brady in Command

With Tom as the starting quarterback, the Patriots were not invincible. They won when it counted, though. They finished the regular season with an 11-5 record—a huge improvement over the previous year's losing season. The Patriots finished as champions of the AFC East. This gave them a spot in the playoffs.

New England's first playoff game was held in a driving snowstorm. The snow did not rattle the Patriots, but their opponent, the Oakland Raiders, did. The Raiders had a 13-3 lead in the fourth quarter before Tom and the New England offense were able to rally for a touchdown to cut the lead to 13-10.

With less than two minutes left, New England got the ball back. With time running out, Tom tried to move his team into field goal range. On one **play**, Tom was hit hard and dropped the ball. A Raiders' player recovered, and it looked as though the Patriots' season was over. But the team caught a huge break. The referees ruled that Tom had been trying to pass, and so the play was ruled an incomplete pass, rather than a **fumble**.

Tom made the most of his second opportunity. He completed a 13-yard pass on the next play. With just 27 seconds left, New England's kicker, Adam Vinatieri, booted a 45-yard field goal through the **uprights** to tie the game and send it into overtime. In the overtime period, the Patriots won the toss, drove 61 yards, and Vinatieri kicked another field goal for a 16-13 win.

Big Hits, Tough Decisions

In the AFC Championship game, the Patriots faced the Pittsburgh Steelers. During the game, Pittsburgh's attacking defense dealt Tom the hardest blow he had suffered all season. Steelers' safety Lee Flowers knocked him to the turf, and Tom had to leave the game with a sprained ankle. Drew Bledsoe played for the first time since the second week of the season. The former starter led the Patriots to a 24-17 victory and into the Super Bowl.

This exciting win was soon tempered by a hard choice for Coach Belichick. Bledsoe naturally wanted to start in the Super Bowl, but Tom had played well all season. When it became clear that Tom's ankle would be fine, the coach chose him to start.

Now the only thing he had to worry about was beating the St. Louis Rams. But this would not be easy. The Rams had finished with a 14-2 record, and had scored more points than any other team in the NFL. Their offense was so powerful, it was called the "Greatest Show on Turf." But Tom took the pressure in stride. Just before the game was to start, a team trainer found him taking a nap. Tom later told a *Boston Globe* reporter,

> **"I fell asleep, and when I woke up, I said to myself I didn't think I'd feel this good. I convinced myself that it was just a game, just another game."**

Tom may have been one of the few people on New England's side who felt so composed. The Patriots were clearly the underdogs. Some experts had picked the Rams to win by more than two touchdowns.

An Upset Victory

When the Patriots took the field in New Orleans for Super Bowl XXXVI, their defense attacked and stifled the Rams. By the middle of the second quarter, St. Louis had managed only a field goal. With the Patriots holding a 7-3 lead, Tom led a **drive** that ended when he found David Patten in the **end zone** with 31 seconds left in the half. When the Patriots went to the locker room up 14-3, it was the first time all season the Rams had fallen behind by more than eight points.

After intermission, the Rams defense toughened. All the Patriots could manage in the third quarter was a field goal. In the last period, Warner drove the Rams downfield, then punched the ball across the goal line himself to cut the deficit to 17-10. The Rams scored again on their next drive. With 1:30 to play, the score was knotted at 17. The Patriots began the last drive on their own 17 yard line.

As confetti swirls down onto the field, Tom celebrates the Patriots' upset victory over the St. Louis Rams in Super Bowl XXXVI. Tom completed 16 of 27 passes for 145 yards and a touchdown. He was named the game's MVP.

The Patriots chose to go for the win. Tom lofted three passes to receiver J. R. Redmon and another to Troy Brown. He sent the last pass to Jermaine Wiggins, who was tackled on the Rams' 30. Tom then raced to the **line of scrimmage** and spiked the ball to stop the clock with seven seconds left. Vinatieri then kicked the ball through the uprights to snatch a 20-17 Super Bowl win.

The Patriots had gone from being one of the weakest teams in the league to world champions. Tom Brady won the Most Valuable Player award, becoming at 24 the youngest quarterback in history to win a Super Bowl. In less than four months he had gone from being an obscure backup to an NFL superstar.

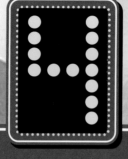

CAPTAIN OF A NEW DYNASTY

In the world of professional football, no player is more admired than a winning quarterback. Tom Brady seemed tailor-made for stardom. Not only was he a good football player, he was also a good-looking guy. In interviews Tom seemed to be modest and easygoing—the kind of person others would like as a friend.

After the Patriots won their first Super Bowl, Tom became an instant celebrity. His picture appeared on a box of Wheaties cereal. He went to Disney World, where he rode in a parade with Mickey Mouse. He attended a victory rally in Boston, waving to cheering crowds that had turned out despite the freezing weather. He served as a judge for the Miss USA Pageant. Soon, *People* magazine named him one of its 50 Most Beautiful People.

Fans wait in line to get Tom Brady's autograph between practice sessions at Patriots' training camp. After winning the Super Bowl in February 2002, Tom was in great demand. Despite the public attention, Tom remained focused on football.

All of a sudden, Tom could not go anywhere without members of the media following him or people begging for his autograph. He signed as many autographs as he could, knowing that pleasing fans is part of being an NFL star.

Big companies recognized Tom's appeal, and soon he was being paid to appear in commercials. He did advertisements for Nike, Sirius satellite radio, the candy company Hershey's, and the clothing store The Gap. He joked that he had to choose the right ads to appear in, for if he looked dumb on screen, he would take a ribbing from his teammates. He was fine with the commercials, though, as long as they did not distract him from his real job. He said,

Tom lunges forward for a first down during a 2003 game against the New York Jets. The 2003 Patriots won 14 games during the regular season. Their record gave New England home-field advantage throughout the playoffs.

> **"The most important thing for me is to be able to win football games and to make sure nothing gets in the way of that. I think all of the decisions off the field are based with that goal in mind, so if you are going to be too involved with a company or your time commitments, you better make sure you are getting your work done."**

On-Field Disappointment

The Patriots did not immediately follow up on their Super Bowl success. In the 2002 season, Tom led the league with 28 touchdown passes, but also established a career high for **interceptions**, with 14. His **quarterback efficiency rating** dropped to 85.7, well below the previous year. In part, Tom's efficiency fell because he played most of the second half of the season with a shoulder injury. Although the team had started out strong, winning its first three games, the Patriots finished the season 9-7 and missed the playoffs.

Tom felt the sting of losing. He said the season had seemed like a long one, for everyone on the team. He said,

> **"These weeks go on, and I think a lot of times in the end of the year a lot of guys are just playing, you know, you're just playing on the vapor. You know, there is no gas in the tank left."**

A Strong Season

Tom and the Patriots regained their stride in a near-perfect 2003 season. At first, things didn't go well, as New England started out 2-2. But the Patriots won their next 12 games to finish with the best record in the AFC, 14-2.

In their divisional playoff game, the Patriots faced a tough opponent in the Tennessee Titans. The Titans were led by an excellent quarterback, Steve McNair. The Patriots scored on the opening drive, but McNair quickly rallied the Titans to tie the game. The contest was tied at 14 in the fourth quarter, but with time running out Brady marched the Patriots into field goal range. Adam Vinatieri booted the winning points with 4:06 left to play.

The AFC Championship again pitted the Patriots against the Indianapolis Colts. With Peyton Manning leading the Colts offense, the game was billed as a true battle of quarterbacks. By the numbers, the All-Pro Manning had been the best quarterback in the league during the regular season, throwing for over 4,200 yards and 29 touchdowns. But the Patriots defense rattled Manning, intercepting him four times. It was one of the worst games of Manning's career. New England's 24-14 victory was its 14th straight win of the season.

New England was on its way to its second Super Bowl under Tom Brady. Tom praised his team, and credited great focus in practice to success on the field. He told a reporter,

"To win 14 in a row, that's unbelievable. I mean, who does that? Nobody does that, and it's great will and great determination, and the preparation will lead to execution on game day by everyone."

An Exciting Super Bowl

The Patriots' opponent in Super Bowl XXXVIII had never before appeared in the big game. Before the 2003 season began, few football experts thought the Carolina Panthers were among the NFL's best teams. After all, they had gone 1-15 and 7-9 the previous two seasons. But led by young quarterback Jake Delhomme, the Panthers had performed beyond expectations, finishing the regular season with an 11-5 record. The team had a reputation for winning close games, just as the Patriots did. Their defense attacked, **sacked**, and stifled opposing quarterbacks.

When the Super Bowl began, neither team's offense was able to score for most of the first half. Only in the final three minutes of the half was Tom able to get the Patriots on the scoreboard, but he did fire two touchdowns as the end of the half neared. The Panthers offense came to life at almost the same time. At halftime, New England led 14-10.

Stingy defenses hobbled both team's quarterbacks during a scoreless third period. Early in the fourth, Brady and Delhomme each threw touchdown passes. After a Carolina defender intercepted Brady, Delhomme fired the longest play from scrimmage in Super

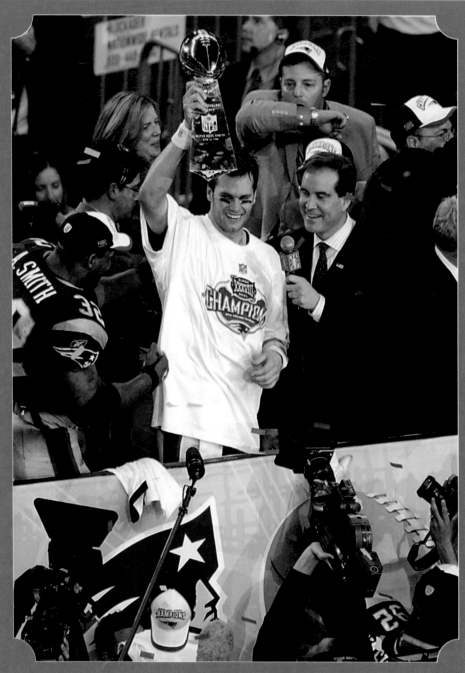

Tom Brady hoists the Lombardi trophy after New England's hard-fought 32-29 victory in Super Bowl XXXVIII. Tom passed for 354 yards and three touchdowns. He also set a Super Bowl record for most passes completed, with 32.

Bowl history, an 85-yard strike to Muhsin Muhammad that put the Panthers ahead, 22-21, with 6:53 to play.

The seesaw contest came down to the last minute with the score tied at 29. Tom looked as cool and confident as if the game were a preseason contest as he marched the team to the Carolina 29-yard line in five plays. With four seconds left in the game, Tom spiked the ball, jogging to the sidelines as Vinatieri ran onto the field. Tom watched from the sidelines with his helmet off as the kick sailed over the Panthers' outstretched hands.

Vinatieri raised his fist in triumph as the ball floated through the uprights. The Patriots had won their second Super Bowl. For the second time, Tom had won the championship game with a drive in the final minute. Once again, he received the MVP award. Tom seemed dazzled by his success, admitting to *USA Today*,

"I can't put it into perspective. I don't know how to feel. You work so hard to get here and do it. I don't know, man, there's a lot of things going through my mind."

Taking a Break

Tom took some time to sort things out after the hoopla of the Patriots' second NFL championship. He traveled to England alone and spent a week touring London. Then his new girlfriend, actress Bridget Moynahan, joined him in Europe. They went to Paris, Florence, and Rome.

For the most part, Tom was less recognized in Europe, where soccer is a bigger draw than American football. Being able to walk the streets without being mobbed was a delight to the quarterback.

Back in the United States, Tom's relationship with Moynahan, a well-known actress and model, became a regular item of gossip news. It was becoming harder to carve out any private time at all and even harder to please people. One day Tom signed autographs for a huge crowd outside the locker room until he had to leave. As he walked away, he heard one disappointed man call him a jerk. He later told the story to a *Washington Post* journalist, adding,

CROSS-CURRENTS

If you'd like to learn more about Tom Brady's girlfriend at the time, read "Bridget Moynahan." Go to page 53. ▶▶

A celebrity photographer snapped this shot of Tom with his girlfriend, Bridget Moynahan. Bridget, an actress, has appeared in such films as *I, Robot* (2004) and *Lord of War* (2005). Tom and Bridget dated from 2004 until late 2006.

❝Do you pay attention to that, being a person that people always look at? It can be very demoralizing.❞

NFL Dynasty

But the Patriots' continuing dominance increased the spotlight on everyone, particularly on their star quarterback. New England lost only twice in the 2004 regular season, finishing with an AFC-best 14-2

The Patriots wait for their quarterback to lead them onto the field before a 2004 game. Defeating the Philadelphia Eagles in Super Bowl XXXIX ensured the Patriots' place as one of the greatest NFL dynasties.

record. Tom had another good year, completing more than 60 percent of his passes for 28 touchdowns and 3,692 yards.

In the divisional playoff, the Patriots held the high-powered Indianapolis offense to just a field goal in a 20-3 victory. In the AFC Championship game, the Patriots had to face their toughest regular season opponent: the Pittsburgh Steelers, who had handed the Patriots their first loss of the season, 34-20, in week eight. The Steelers did not look nearly as impressive in the rematch, as the Patriots clobbered them, 41-27.

Again, Tom Brady and his Patriots were bound for the Super Bowl. There they would face the Philadelphia Eagles. Tom and Eagles quarterback Donovan McNabb were friends off the field, but McNabb was cold-blooded with the ball in his hands. He was mobile in the pocket and able to coolly complete long passes on third and fourth **downs**. The Eagles had lost in the NFC Championship game three times before finally breaking through in 2004 to reach the Super Bowl for the second time in team history.

Eagles fans seemed predominant in the crowd of 78,125 at Alltel Stadium in Jacksonville, Florida. At least they were louder. Philadelphia scored first on a nine-play, 81-yard drive. But the Patriots soon responded with a touchdown of their own.

As the fourth quarter began, the game was tied at 14-14. But Tom led New England on two scoring drives to open up a 24-14 lead. Although the Eagles threatened, McNabb couldn't quite pull off the comeback. New England won its third Super Bowl in four years by a 24-21 score. As with the victory over the Panthers the year before, it had been no trouncing—just enough to make history.

The Patriots had now become the dominant team of their decade, just as the San Francisco 49ers had dominated the 1980s of Tom's childhood. Like any dynasty, New England's players had also put targets on their backs for every other team around the league. The pressure would only mount as writers and fans began to wonder if the Patriots could be the best team ever to play the game.

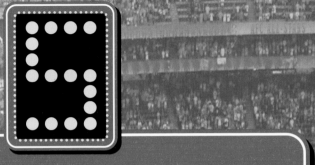

QUEST FOR PERFECTION

For the next few seasons, the Patriots remained among the NFL's best teams. They won the AFC East title in 2005 with a 10-6 regular-season record. They won the title again in 2006 with a 12-4 mark. However, both years the Patriots lost in the playoffs, and did not reach the Super Bowl.

Tom continued to be one of the league's best quarterbacks. In 2005, injuries to several New England running backs meant that he had to throw the ball more than ever before. He passed for a league-leading 4,110 yards and had 26 touchdown passes. After the season ended, it was revealed that Tom had played with an injury in December and January. In 2006, Tom passed for more than 3,500 yards and 24 touchdowns. Under his leadership, in the playoffs New England had beaten the San Diego Chargers,

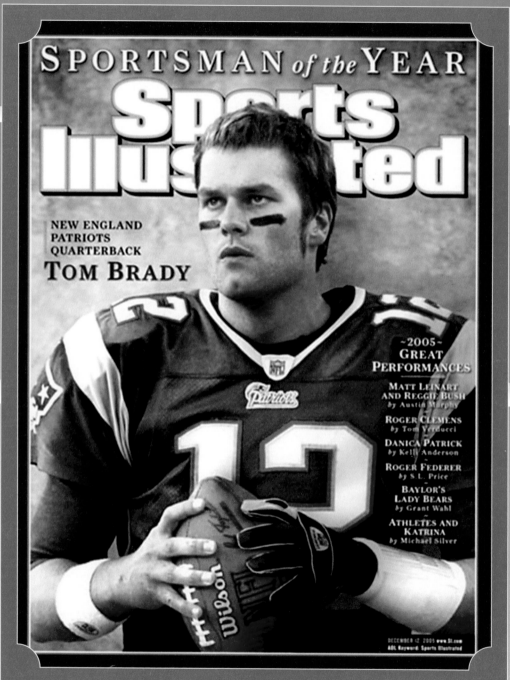

Sports Illustrated named Tom "Sportsman of the Year" in 2005. "The guy really plays with fire," wrote sportswriter Peter King. "Don't be surprised if he wins more Sportsman awards and more Super Bowls in the years to come."

who had been favored to win the AFC. However, the next week the Patriots lost to their rivals, the Indianapolis Colts, who went on to win the Super Bowl.

Before the 2007 season began, the Patriots made some moves to improve their teams. They signed speedy wide receivers Randy Moss and Donte Stallworth. Over the years, Tom had never really had a superstar wide receiver on his team. Now, he had two excellent pass-catchers he could throw to. Most of the experts proclaimed New England the team to beat.

A New Arrival

Tom had some changes in his personal life as well. In December 2006, he broke up with Bridget Moynahan. By the summer of 2007, he was dating Gisele Bündchen, a supermodel who had been born in Brazil.

Bündchen had appeared on the covers of the most prestigious fashion magazines, including *Vogue*, *Elle*, and *Allure*. She was the highest-paid model in the world, having accumulated a $150 million fortune by the time she met Tom.

CROSS-CURRENTS

If you would like to learn more about the career of Tom Brady's supermodel girlfriend, check out "Gisele Bündchen." Go to page 54. ▶▶

But it turned out Tom would have a permanent connection with Moynahan. On August 22, 2007, the actress gave birth to a baby boy. The child was Tom's. He was happy about the birth of his son. Tom called the birth a "a very joyous, happy situation." However, his relationship with Moynahan had become strained. Tom did not attend the birth, and the boy bore his mother's last name: John Edward Thomas Moynahan.

Unstoppable Force

In the 2007 season, Tom Brady and the Patriots found that winning can create just as much stress as losing. As the Patriots downed foe after foe, the media began to speculate that New England could go through the entire season unbeaten. Tom's excellence on the field added to the mounting "perfect season" pressure from fans and the press. He broke records all season long, and appeared almost invincible, finding his receivers with cool accuracy.

Throughout the season, the Patriots faced opponents that provided crucial tests of their strength. One of the first was Dallas, in the fifth week. Both teams were undefeated, and some analysts predicted the two could meet in the Super Bowl. The Patriots did not just defeat the Cowboys, they destroyed them, 48-27. Tom fired 31 completions in 46 attempts, passed for 388 yards, and hit five receivers for touchdowns. The aerial show he staged in Dallas marked the best game of his career.

Reporters wanted to talk about his five touchdown passes, which set a team record, but Tom wanted to talk about the team. In the post-game press conference, he said:

During the 2007 season, opposing defenses found that they could not stop Tom, pictured here calling a play at the line of scrimmage. Tom's favorite targets in 2007 included All-Pro wide receivers Randy Moss and Wes Welker.

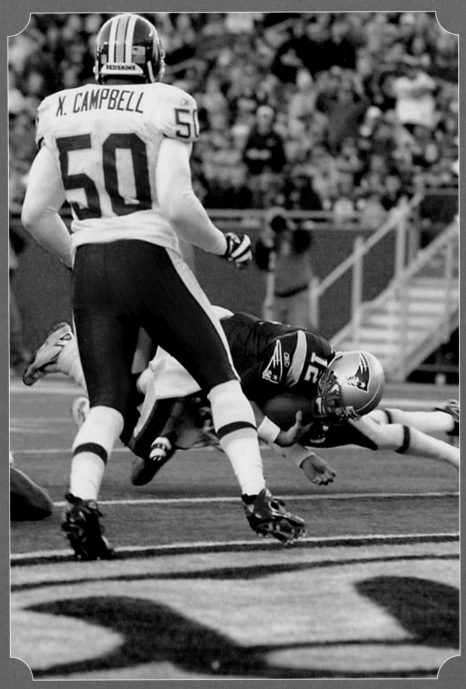

Tom dives into the end zone for a touchdown during an October 2007 game against the Washington Redskins. New England's easy 52-7 victory improved the Patriots' season record to 8-0.

> **"The touchdown passes are not very important. I think winning the game is most important. . . . I'd love to set plenty of team records. But the individual records are based on opportunities you get. . . . It's just a touchdown for our offense and that's what I get excited about."**

Another tough test came against the Indianapolis Colts in the ninth game. The Colts were not only the defending Super Bowl champs, but also unbeaten. It was a road game for the Patriots, and the large, loud, and hostile crowd booed as Tom took the field. The Colts defense swarmed over Brady's receivers, forcing two interceptions. Indianapolis held a 10-point lead by the fourth quarter. However, Tom managed to lead a comeback, bringing his team back for a 24-20 win.

Too Close for Comfort

After this win, everyone was gunning for the Patriots. Even losing teams tried their hardest to beat them. In the team's 13th game, the Patriots faced the Baltimore Ravens, who had won only four games all year. But the Ravens came to life against the Patriots. Once again, it took last minute heroics from the quarterback to salvage the win. The Patriots trailed 24-20 with barely more than three minutes left when Tom and his receivers mounted a game winning drive, marked by do-or-die fourth-down completions. The Patriots narrowly eked out a 27-24 win.

In the last game of the regular season, the Patriots faced the toughest brawl they had played in all year. The New York Giants' defense sealed up the line of scrimmage, preventing Tom from making short passes. Giants quarterback Eli Manning helped turn the game into an offensive shootout, and at half-time, the Patriots went into their locker room trailing 21-16.

The game rocked back and forth as both Brady and Manning fought out a battle of quarterbacks. During the furious struggle, Tom broke the NFL's single-season record for touchdown passes with his 50th, on a pass to Moss. However, the contest remained tight. The Giants scored a late touchdown to cut the Patriots' lead to three

CROSS-CURRENTS

To find out about a controversy that threatened to derail the Patriots' perfect season, read "Spygate."

Go to page 55. ▶▶

Eli Manning of the New York Giants (number 10) looks to pass during the final regular-season game of 2007. Although the Giants played hard, the Patriots won, 38-35, and finished the season with an undefeated 16-0 record.

points with a minute to play. But the Patriots were able to run out the clock and seal the win. They had become the first NFL team to finish the regular season 16-0.

Road to the Super Bowl

The Patriots had little trouble in their first two playoff games. In the divisional playoffs, New England easily beat the Jacksonville Jaguars, 31-20. In the game, Tom set an NFL record for best completion percentage in a game. He completed 26 of 28 passes—92.8 percent—passing for 268 yards and three touchdowns. The next week, the San Diego Chargers could manage only four field goals in New England's 21-12 victory.

The Patriots were on their way to the Super Bowl—and so were the Giants. New York earned its trip to the big game in Glendale, Arizona, by winning three playoff games on the road, including an upset victory over the Green Bay Packers in the NFC Championship game.

During the two weeks before the Super Bowl, questions briefly swirled around Tom's health. Photographers shot pictures of him walking with a cast on his right foot when he and Gisele Bündchen were entering her New York apartment. He was also seen limping. It turned out to be a false alarm, for he soon appeared in public without the cast and with no limp.

The run-up to the game was the usual media carnival. Reporters peppered Brady with questions about his apparent injury and the Patriots' so-far perfect season. One journalist even showed up in a wedding dress and jokingly asked him to marry her.

The circus ended on game day. From the start, Super Bowl XLII was a game dominated by the defenses—not a good sign for a team so dependent on offense like the Patriots. Giants defenders brought enormous pressure on Brady, sacking him five times throughout the course of the game. The first half ended with the Patriots ahead 7-3. Tom's offense had been held to just 81 yards.

A Giant Upset

The Giants defenders continued to pressure Tom in the second half while shutting down his receivers' routes. Both quarterbacks struggled. Neither team could score in the third quarter. In the

In Super Bowl XLII, New York's defense succeeded in pressuring Tom Brady and interrupting the flow of New England's offense. Although Tom passed for 266 yards and a touchdown, he was also sacked five times during the game.

fourth quarter, the Giants finally scored a touchdown to take a 10-7 lead.

The Patriots were not finished, though. With less than three minutes left, Tom found Randy Moss in the end zone for a touchdown that put the Patriots back on top, 14-10. But on the next possession, Manning managed to escape heavy pressure from New England. On one play he completed a long pass to David Tyree. A few moments later Manning delivered the ball into the hands of Plaxico Burress for a touchdown, putting New York up 17-14.

Plaxico Burress (number 17) pulls in a 13-yard touchdown pass to give the Giants a 17-14 lead with 35 seconds left in Super Bowl XLII. The game would be remembered as one of the biggest upsets in NFL history.

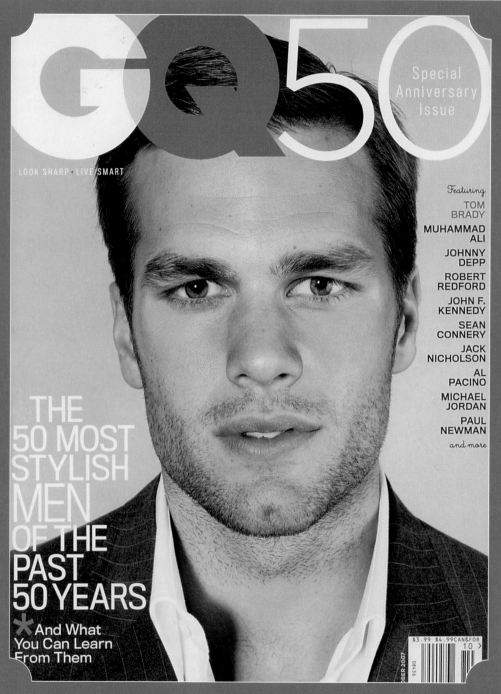

GQ magazine chose Tom Brady for the cover of its 50th anniversary issue in 2007 because of his Super Bowl success. But Tom was also praised in the magazine for his charity work and leadership.

The Patriots got the ball back with 29 seconds left. This time, however, they were not able to manage a last-minute comeback. Tom was sacked again, threw two desperation passes, and the game ended.

In a press conference after the game, Tom admitted the loss had been extremely painful. The "perfect season" had ended one victory short of perfection. New England had also missed a chance to establish itself as the equal of the 1970s Pittsburgh Steelers or the 1980s San Francisco 49ers—dynasties that had each won four Super Bowls. Yet Tom had praise for the Giants, saying of the defeat,

"But it is just part of competition; we competed against a team that is very deserving of being Super Bowl champs."

Time Enough to Win

Tom Brady has achieved a lot thus far in his career. He is just the fourth player in Super Bowl history to earn multiple MVP awards. He is the winningest quarterback in Patriots history, and the only one in the history of the NFL to win three Super Bowls before his 28th birthday. He holds numerous NFL records.

In the run-up to Super Bowl XLII, one reporter asked Tom what his purpose in life was. Tom stressed his good fortune, saying,

"We are blessed to have the opportunity to live out, truly, childhood dreams. People say living a dream, but we truly are living a dream. All of us grew up and you wanted to be a professional athlete. All of us wanted to play in a Super Bowl, and to have this spectacle and to enjoy this and to have this experience, we are going to remember this for the rest of our lives."

Tom Brady still loves the game as much as he did when he was a kid. At the age of 30, he has plenty of football left in him. He is the rare player born to be a quarterback and will likely be calling the signals every game day for years to come.

Undefeated Dolphins

The 1972 Miami Dolphins are the only team in NFL history to go undefeated for an entire season. At the time, NFL teams played 14 games, rather than the 16 that are played today. Miami won all of its regular-season games, two playoff games, and Super Bowl VII.

Coach Don Shula was in his third year as Miami's head coach when the Dolphins' run began. Their team had many star players. Quarterback Bob Griese—whose son Brian would later play with Tom Brady at the University of Michigan—went on to the Hall of Fame, as did Larry Csonka, Larry Little, Nick Buoniconti, Jim Langer, and Paul Warfield. But the Dolphins also had many role players. Miami's defensive unit was nicknamed the "No-Name Defense" because so many lesser-known players made big plays.

Quarterback Earl Morrall became part of the legend when he came off the bench to replace an injured Griese in the fifth week of the season. Morrall was 38, very old by the standards of professional football. But he kept the streak alive through the rest of the season, and won a playoff game against Cleveland. The next week, Griese returned to lead the Dolphins past the Pittsburgh Steelers. The Dolphins finished their historic journey with a 14-7 triumph over the Washington Redskins in Super Bowl VII.

(Go back to page 6.)

Joe Montana

Joe Montana was one of Tom Brady's childhood idols—perhaps the single player Tom most wanted to be like. Montana, who was known for his ability to stay calm under pressure, spent most of his professional career playing for the San Francisco 49ers. The team played at Candlestick Park, where the Brady family attended NFL games. Montana was one of the greatest pro football players of all time.

During the 1980s, Montana became famous for his ability to lead comebacks against great odds. He could pull close games out at the last minute. One such game was the first game Tom remembers seeing, the 1981 NFC Championship Game. Trailing the Dallas Cowboys 27-21, Montana's 49ers drove to the 6-yard line. Despite a furious rush from Cowboy defenders and having his intended receiver covered, Montana managed to loft a pass to Dwight Clark in the back of the end zone. Football fans still remember Clark's famous reception as "The Catch."

Joe Montana was born in New Eagle, Pennsylvania, the son of Joseph and Theresa Montana. He grew up in Monongahela, a small town near Pittsburgh. He faced many of the obstacles Tom did in getting into the game of football, including the belief of others that he was too small. He played football, baseball, and basketball at Ringgold High School.

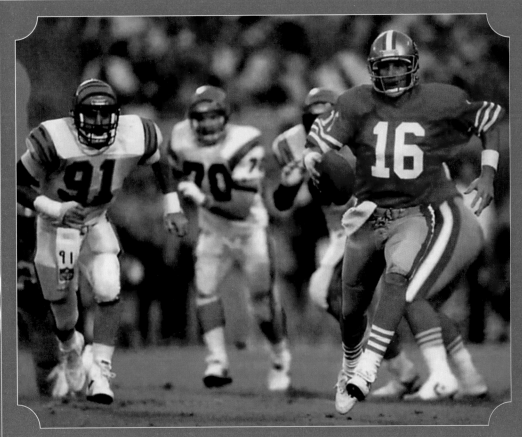

San Francisco 49ers quarterback Joe Montana (number 16) runs away from Bengals defenders during Super Bowl XXIII (1989). Montana led the 49ers to victory that day; it was the third of his four Super Bowl titles.

He attended Notre Dame University, where he became part of one of the best football programs in the country. He struggled at first to get playing time, but eventually worked his way to starting quarterback. In 1978, he helped lead the Fighting Irish to a national championship.

Montana began his career with the 49ers in 1979, and played there for the next fourteen seasons. Five times he was rated the best quarterback in the National Football Conference. He led the 49ers to four Super Bowl victories during the 1980s, and three times was the Most Valuable Player in the game. Montana was voted the NFL's Most Valuable Player in 1989 and 1990. Eight times, he was selected for the Pro Bowl.

In 1993, Montana was traded to the Kansas City Chiefs, and played two seasons there before retiring. In 2000, Joe Montana was elected to the Pro Football Hall of Fame. In 2006, *Sports Illustrated* called him the greatest clutch quarterback of all time. (Go back to page 11.) ◀◀

Wolverines Football

The University of Michigan, where Tom Brady attended college, has one of the strongest football programs in the United States. The school began competing in 1879, making it one of the first colleges to play football. The Wolverines have won or shared 11 national championships. They also hold the national record for games won, with more than 860.

During football season, Saturdays in the university town of Ann Arbor are raucous celebrations, where the streets swell with people wearing Michigan's colors. The air is filled with the sound of rock music and the smell from tailgate barbeque parties. The stadium can seat more than 112,000 people, and games almost always sell out.

Michigan's fiercest rival is Ohio State. Both teams play in the Big Ten Conference, and the game is almost always the last one on their schedules. The game has frequently determined the Big Ten champion. Other big rivals include Michigan State, Notre Dame, Penn State, and the University of Minnesota.

Lloyd Carr, who coached Tom Brady at Michigan, led the team from 1995 to 2008. During his time as Michigan's coach, his teams won five Big Ten crowns and shared the national title in 1997. The Associated Press ranked Michigan among its Top 25 college football teams for all but nine of the team's games under Coach Carr. (Go back to page 13.) ◀◀

Coach Belichick

Bill Belichick of the Patriots has coached longer than any other active coach, with 33 years in the pros. Patriots fans know him as a man who praises opposing teams, downplays his own team's successes, and rarely smiles during games or press conferences. These things are all part of a strategy he uses to keep players motivated. He knows that if expectations are high, they can work in a rival team's favor. He's been called a genius—even a "mad scientist"—for his ability to extract the best performance from his squads.

Belichick was born in Nashville, Tennessee, on April 16, 1952. He was raised in Annapolis, Maryland. Football ran in his family. His father Steve played fullback for the Detroit Lions, and later coached at the Naval Academy. Bill was an outstanding player at the high school level, and he is honored in Annapolis High's Hall of Fame. He went to college at Wesleyan, and earned a degree in economics in 1975.

He worked as an assistant coach for the Baltimore Colts, Detroit Lions and Denver Broncos. For twelve years, he was an assistant coach with the New York Giants, working with both defense and special teams, before being named defensive coordinator in 1985. Belichick's first opportunity as a head coach came in 1991, when he took over the Cleveland

Browns. However, his time there was largely disappointing. In five seasons, the Browns managed just a 36-44 record. Belichick also angered fans when he cut popular quarterback Bernie Kosar in 1993, replacing him with Vinny Testaverde. Belichick ended his career with the Browns during dark days for Cleveland fans. After the team finished 5-11 in 1995, owner Art Modell moved the franchise to Baltimore, Maryland.

After being fired by the franchise (now the Baltimore Ravens) in 1996, Belichick held several assistant coaching jobs. In 2000, he was hired as the Patriots' head coach, and one of the first players drafted under his leadership was Tom Brady. Since then, Belichick has established himself as one of the best coaches in NFL He is the only coach in the league to win three Super Bowls in four years. His teams have also set several records for win streaks, including consecutive overall wins (21), consecutive regular season wins (18), and consecutive playoff wins. (Go back to page 18.)

Over the past decade, Bill Belichick has emerged as one of the National Football League's most successful head coaches. He was named NFL Coach of the Year in 2003 and 2007.

The New England Patriots

The New England Patriots became one of the National Football League's most powerful teams under Tom Brady's leadership. But the team faced many years of struggle before it finally gained success.

The Patriots came into existence in 1959, when a group of local businessmen led by William H. "Billy" Sullivan Jr. succeeded in having the Boston-based club accepted into the American Football League (AFL). It was the eighth and last team admitted into the AFL, one of two professional football leagues in America at the time. A public contest was held to name the squad, which first played as the Boston Patriots.

The Patriots played their first games at Boston University Field. Lou Saban was the team's first head coach. A Patriots defensive player, Bob Dee, recovered a fumble and scored the team's first touchdown in a game against the Buffalo Bills. Throughout the 1960s, the Patriots produced outstanding players but did not earn a championship. In 1970, the AFL merged with the National Football League and the Patriots became an NFL squad in the American Football Conference.

Today, the New England Patriots play their home games at Gillette Stadium in Foxborough, Massachusetts. The 68,000-seat stadium opened in 2002. Since then, the Patriots have won more than 80 percent of their home games.

The Patriots barely had a home in their first decade. They moved from Boston University Field to Harvard Stadium, Fenway Park, and Boston College Alumni Stadium. In 1970, the team moved from Boston to Foxboro. The next year, the team's name was changed to the New England Patriots.

During the 1970s and 1980s, the Patriots never won a championship, although the team continued to produce its share of stars. One of these was John Hannah, an offensive tackle who was eventually elected to the Pro Football Hall of Fame. In 1978, the Patriots won the first division title in their history, but lost to the Houston Oilers in their first home playoff game. In 1985, New England won its first trip to the Super Bowl. However, its opponent was the powerful Chicago Bears, considered one of the greatest NFL teams of all time. The Bears routed the Patriots, 46-10—at the time, the most one-sided game in Super Bowl history.

In January 1994, Robert K. Kraft became the team's fourth owner. Kraft was an amiable person, well-liked by fans, and he promised them the Patriots would win a championship within ten years.

The Patriots delivered on that promise after the 2001 season, Tom Brady's first as starting quarterback. He led the team to a Super Bowl triumph over the heavily favored Rams. Brady's Patriots delivered two more Super Bowl victories in the next three years, with wins over the Carolina Panthers and the Philadelphia Eagles. (Go back to page 18.) ◀◀

Bridget Moynahan

Today Bridget Moynahan is famous because of her work as a model and actress. But when she was growing up, she had something in common with future boyfriend Tom Brady. She was athletic, playing basketball, lacrosse, and soccer in high school. She did not even read fashion magazines.

She was born Kathryn Bridget Moynahan on April 28, 1971, in Binghamton, New York. Bridget was raised in Longmeadow, Massachusetts. Her father was a scientist, her mother a schoolteacher. She attended Longmeadow High School, and graduated in 1989.

Bridget's modeling career started as something of a fluke. A friend of hers asked to go along on a modeling tryout. Her friend did not get a job offer, but Moynahan did.

Moynahan studied acting at Caymichael Patten Studio in New York City. The studio honed her acting skills and prepared her for the pressures of the business. In 1999 she landed a break when she was hired to play Natasha in the television show *Sex and the City*. She got another prominent role in the movie *Coyote Ugly* in 2000. After this, Moynahan earned roles in a string of hit movies, including *The Sum of All Fears*, *The Recruit*, *Lord of War*, and *I, Robot*.

(Go back to page 32.)

Gisele Bündchen

Tom Brady's supermodel girlfriend does not need to envy his salary as an NFL quarterback. Gisele Bündchen is the highest-paid model in the world, with $35 million in earnings in 2008.

She was born in 1980 in Três de Maio, Brazil. Her father worked in a bank, her mother as a writer and teacher at a university. Like Tom, she was raised a Catholic. Gisele is still

more popular in her native country than anywhere else, although she has achieved international fame. After a Brazilian clothing company hired her, their sales went up 20 percent. Gisele has signed deals worth millions of dollars from companies like Bulgari, Dolce & Gabbana, and Victoria's Secret.

Gisele is active in many social causes, including the fight against AIDS and world hunger. She joined with rock musician Bono of U2 to help raise money for African AIDS victims. She has served as a spokeswoman for breast cancer research, and has donated profits from her line of sandals to help save the Amazon rain forest.

Gisele has also seen her share of controversy. She was criticized by some people for her refusal to accept United States dollars for her work, after the dollar fell in value against other world currencies.

(Go back to page 38.)

On her Web site, Brazilian supermodel Gisele Bündchen explains that her dreams include "to build a family as wonderful as my own" and to "see a world without [hunger] and war."

Spygate

In 2007 an event that occurred early in the Patriots' run toward an undefeated regular season became a national controversy. It was called "Spygate" by the media, and threatened the team's ability to stay focused on winning a championship.

In their 2007 season opener, the Patriots crushed the Jets, 38-14. The victory was not a surprise. New England had been favored to win. But after the game, Jets officials complained to the league that a member of the Patriots staff had violated NFL rules. The Patriots had sent someone to the sidelines to videotape the Jets' coaching staff's defensive signals during the game. The Jets had confronted the assistant and confiscated his camera during the game.

When this evidence was revealed, the National Football League officially charged the Patriots with breaking the rules. The league fined Coach Belichick $500,000, fined the Patriots another $250,000, and stripped the team of a first-round pick in the 2008 draft. Belichick's fine was the highest ever imposed on a coach.

The media began to refer to the incident as "Spygate." The name came from "Watergate," the name of the Washington hotel burglarized by men working for President Richard Nixon in 1972, as they attempted to put eavesdropping equipment in his political opponents' headquarters. The scandal that resulted as the involvement of Nixon's men was uncovered forced the president to resign in disgrace in 1974. Since then, the press has often added the term "-gate" to public scandals.

Few fans or reporters considered the videotaping a major factor in the Patriots' success, but it was a serious violation of the rules. Two days after the game, Belichick issued a public apology. He added that the taping had no effect on the game against the Jets, however, and declared he would not make any other statement about it. Patriots owner Robert Kraft also apologized publicly. Later, both men apologized privately at meetings of NFL coaches and team owners.

After apologizing, Belichick tried to turn the incident to his team's advantage. All the controversy, he told the players, just demonstrated that the media was out to get New England. This proved to be a very effective strategy—typical of Belichick's motivation techniques— and it helped the Patriots return their focus to winning games.

(Go back to page 41.)

1977   Tom Edward Brady Jr. is born on August 3, in San Mateo, California, the son of
Tom Sr. and Galynn Brady.

1994   In Tom's senior football season at Junípero Serra High School, he is named an
All-American by *Blue Chip Illustrated* and *Prep Football Report*.

1995   Enters University of Michigan. Coach Lloyd Carr "redshirts" Tom, making him eligible
to practice, but not to play, with the Wolverines.

1996   He becomes the third-string quarterback for the Wolverines, behind Brian Griese and
Scott Driesbach.

1998   Tom becomes the starting quarterback for Michigan Wolverines. They tie for the
Big Ten championship. In the Citrus Bowl, Tom pulls the offense together for a
come-from-behind victory.

1999   Brady leads the Wolverines to a string of victories, finishing with a win over Alabama
in the Orange Bowl. In that game, Brady shatters Orange Bowl records, with
46 passing attempts, 31 completions, 369 yards, and four touchdowns.

2000   Tom is the 199th player picked in the National Football League draft. He begins the
season as New England's fourth-string quarterback.

2001   Tom becomes the backup quarterback, behind starter Drew Bledsoe. In the second
game, he becomes the starter when Bledsoe suffers a severe chest injury.

2002   On February 3, Brady leads the Patriots to a 20-17 win over the heavily favored
Rams in Super Bowl XXXVI. He is named the game's Most Valuable Player.

2004   On February 1, Brady leads New England past the Carolina Panthers, 31-29, in
Super Bowl XXXVIII. He wins his second MVP award.

2005   The Patriots win their third Super Bowl, defeating the Philadelphia Eagles, 24-21.

2006   New England reaches the AFC Championship game, but loses to the Indianapolis Colts.

2007   Brady quarterbacks the Patriots through a 16-0 regular season, the first time that
had ever been done. He sets numerous NFL records, including most touchdown
passes in a season (50).

2008   Tom Brady is named the MVP for the NFL. Brady again leads the Patriots to the
Super Bowl, where they are upset by the New York Giants 17-14.

National Football League Most Valuable Player, 2007

Super Bowl Most Valuable Player, 2002, 2004

Pro Bowl, 2002, 2005, 2007, 2008

Most touchdown passes in a season (50)

League leader, touchdown passes, 2002, 2007

Most completions in a Super Bowl (32, 2004)

Most career Super Bowl completions (100)

All-time leader in overtime wins without a defeat (7-0).

Patriots' all-time leader in career completion percentage (61.9 percent) and passer rating (88.4).

Statistics

Year	G	Comp	Att	Pct	Yds	TD	Int	Rating
2000	1	1	3	33.3	6	0	0	42.4
2001	15	264	413	63.9	2,843	18	12	86.5
2002	16	373	601	62.1	3,764	28	14	85.7
2003	16	317	527	60.2	3,620	23	12	85.9
2004	16	288	474	60.8	3,692	28	14	92.6
2005	16	334	530	63.0	4,110	26	14	92.3
2006	16	319	516	61.8	3,529	24	12	87.9
2007	16	398	578	68.9	4,806	50	8	117.2
Total		2,294	3,642	63.0	26,370	197	86	92.9

Books

Boston Globe. *Greatness: The Rise of Tom Brady*. Chicago: Triumph Books, 2006.

Boston Herald. *Tom Brady: Most Valuable Patriot*. Introduction by Stephanie Fuqua. Champaign, Ill.: Sports Publishing, 2002.

Gigliotti, Jim. *Tom Brady*. Mankato, Minn.: Child's World, 2007.

Pierce, Charles P. *Moving the Chains: Tom Brady and the Pursuit of Everything*. New York: Farrar, Straus and Giroux, 2006.

Stewart, Mark. *Tom Brady: Heart of the Huddle*. Brookfield, Conn.: The Millbrook Press, 2003.

Web Sites

http://www.patriots.com

The official site of the New England Patriots is one of the oldest in football, established in 1995. It contains game summaries, press conferences, stats, team records, and more.

http://www.nfl.com

The official site of the National Football League contains information, photos, news stories, game summaries, and schedules for all 32 teams.

http://sports.espn.go.com/nfl/players/profile?statsId=5228

ESPN's site contains information about Tom Brady's career, including his statistics and records.

http://www.sportsline.com/nfl/players/playerpage/187741

The official site for CBS News contains statistics, colorful quotes, and Tom Brady fantasy team analysis.

http://www.boston.com/sports/football/patriots/

This site carries news from the *Boston Globe*, with information about the NFL in general, but with a Patriots Notebook that is a reliable source for up-to-date team information.

attempt—a forward pass thrown by a quarterback.

completion—a pass that is successfully caught by the intended receiver.

defense—the unit of a team which must prevent the other team from moving toward the goal line or scoring.

down—one play, beginning when the center snaps the ball, and ending when the referee calls the ball dead, or in situations when clock cannot be stopped, when the next play begins.

draft—the National Football League's annual selection of new players, usually from colleges and universities.

drive—the series of plays an offense uses to attempt to score, either with a field goal or a touchdown.

end zone—the ten yards between the goal line and the end of the field.

field goal—the three points awarded a team when a kicker kicks the ball through the uprights from any point on the field.

franchise—a team in the National Football League.

fumble—loss of the ball by any offensive player to a defensive player.

interception—the play made when a member of the defense catches a pass intended for a receiver on the offense.

line of scrimmage—the point on the field from which the ball is snapped.

NFL—the National Football League, consisting of 16 teams each in the National Football Conference (NFC) and the American Football Conference (AFC).

offense—the unit of a team which must advance the ball toward the goal line and score, either through touchdowns or field goal.

play—any series of actions taken to accomplish an objective by either the defense or the offense. It may be accomplished by either a group of players, as when an offense attempts a plan to reach the end zone, or by a single player, such as when a defensive player makes an interception or a sack.

Quarterback efficiency rating—a statistic measuring the quality of a quarterback's play, determined through a formula consisting of completion percentage, yards per attempt, touchdowns per attempt, and interceptions per attempt. Also known as passer rating.

redshirt—an athlete who may attend classes and practice with a team, but who may not participate in actual games, thus allowing the official start of a four-year college athletic career to be delayed.

sack—a tackle of the quarterback behind the line of scrimmage.

touchdown—the six points awarded a team for getting the ball into the end zone.

uprights—the two vertical bars on the goal post, through which a ball must be kicked for an extra point or a field goal.

page 4   "To be honest . . ." NFL.com, "Patriots quarterback Brady rides records to MVP Award." http://www.nfl.com/news/story?id=09000d5d805bfaa5

page 8   "I have always . . ." NFL.com, "Patriots quarterback Brady rides records to MVP Award."

page 9   "He's our MVP . . ." NFL.com, "Patriots quarterback Brady rides records to MVP Award."

page 9   "He deserves it . . ." NFL.com, "Patriots quarterback Brady rides records to MVP Award."

page 11   ""I have a special relationship . . ." Sam Blair, "T Is for Team . . . and T is for Tom Brady, the New England Patriots' Sudden Superstar Quarterback," *Boys' Life* 92, no. 9 (September 2002), p. 28.

page 12   "I don't think . . ." Charles P. Pierce, *Moving the Chains: Tom Brady and the Pursuit of Everything* (New York: Farrar, Straus and Giroux, 2006), pp. 35–36.

page 18   "He was really . . ." Pierce, *Moving the Chains*, p. 60.

page 18   "So this skinny . . ." Pierce, *Moving the Chains*, p. 95.

page 21   "You go through . . ." Kevin Paul DuPont, "Poised," in *Greatness: The Rise of Tom Brady* (Chicago: Triumph Books, 2006), p. 59-60.

page 24   "I fell asleep . . . " Bob Ryan, "For Real," in *Greatness: The Rise of Tom Brady*, p. 63.

page 29   "The most important . . ." Darren Rovell, "Brady Careful about What He Endorses," ESPN.com (February 2, 2005). http://sports.espn.go.com/nfl/playoffs04/news/story?id=1982198

page 29   "These weeks go . . ." Bob Ryan, "Weary," in *Greatness: The Rise of Tom Brady*, p. 86.

page 30   "To win 14 . . ." Sean Smith, "The Streak," in *Greatness: The Rise of Tom Brady*, p. 106.

page 32   "I can't put . . ." Jon Saraceno, "Brady's Super Bowl Acumen Reaching Montana-like Status," *USA Today* (February 2, 2004). http://www.usatoday.com/sports/columnist/saraceno/2004-02-02-saraceno_x.htm

page 33   ""Do you pay . . ." Sally Jenkins, "Intentionally Grounded: Pats' Brady Would rather Pass When Attention Comes His Way," Washington Post (January 16, 2005). http://www.washingtonpost.com/wp-dyn/articles/A12588-2005Jan15.html

page 37   "The guy really plays . . ." Peter King, "Many reasons Pats' Brady Earned this Year's Honor," *Sports Illustrated* 103, no. 23 (December 12, 2005), p. 76.

page 41   "The touchdown passes . . ." New England Patriots, "Tom Brady Press Conference" (October 14, 2007). http://www.patriots.com/games/index.cfm?ac=completereportsdetail&pid=28339&pcid=85&special_section=na

page 47   "But it is . . ." New England Patriots, "Tom Brady Press Conference" (February 3, 2008). http://www.patriots.com/games/index.cfm?ac=completereportsdetail&pid=30856&pcid=47&special_section=na

page 47   "We are blessed . . ." . . ." New England Patriots, "Tom Brady Press Conference" (January 29, 2008). http://www.patriots.com/mediacenter/index.cfm?ac=audionewsdetail&pid=30684&pcid=85&rss=1

page 54   "to build a family . . ." Gisele Bündchen, "Dreams." http://www.giselebundchen.com.br/gisele_perfil.asp

Calvin Craig Miller is the author of numerous young adult biographies. His work has been honored by inclusion on the New York Public Library's *Books for the Teen-Age*. In 2006, his biography of civil rights pioneer Bayard Rustin won the Carter G. Woodson Award. He lives in North Carolina.

PICTURE CREDITS

page

5: David Silveman/NEP/SPCS

7: SportsChrome Pix

8: Elsa/Getty Images

11: NFL/Getty Images

14: Detroit Free Press/KRT

17: David Silveman/NEP/SPCS

19: David Silveman/NEP/SPCS

20: David Silveman/NEP/SPCS

22: David Silveman/NEP/SPCS

25: The Boston Globe/KRT

27: David Silveman/NEP/SPCS

28: NEP/SPCS

31: The Dallas Morning News/KRT

33: The Boston Globe/CIC

34: NEP/SPCS

37: Sports Illustrated/NMI

39: Newsday/MCT

40: Keith Nordstrom/NEP/SPCS

42: Newsday/MCT

44: Newsday/MCT

45: Ben Liebenberg/NFL/Getty Images

46: GQ/NMI

49: Rob Brown/NFL Photos

51: AP Photo

52: IOS Photos

54: Fashion Wire Daily

Front cover: Brendan Smialowski/Getty Images
Front cover inset: Peter Ventrone/NEP/SPCS